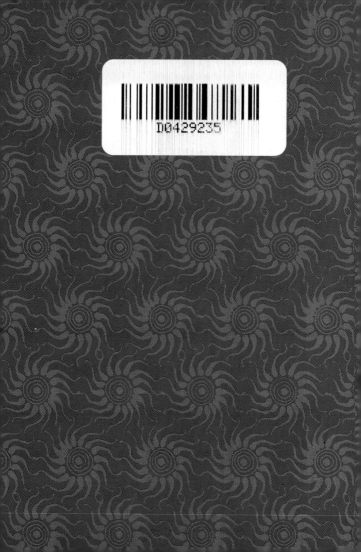

D0429235

I Ching

by Lauren David Peden

THE MYSTICAL ARTS

Illustrations by Jenny Tylden Wright

WARNER ☯ TREASURES

PUBLISHED BY WARNER BOOKS

A TIME WARNER COMPANY

Warner Treasures is a
trademark of Warner Books, Inc.

Warner Books, Inc.,
1271 Avenue of the Americas,
New York, NY 10020

Ⓦ A Time Warner Company

Printed in China
First Printing: March 1996
10 9 8 7 6 5 4 3 2 1

ISBN: 0-446-91013-9

I Ching

THE MYSTICAL ARTS

The *I Ching* is the ancient Chinese oracle of change. In Chinese, the word *I* (pronounced "ee") means "change" and *Ching* means "book"; so the title translates to *Book of Changes*. It is based on the concept that everything in the universe is somehow connected. As the system has evolved, it's become commonplace to ask increasingly complex questions regarding the more difficult dilemmas we face in our everyday lives: "Should I marry so-and-so?" "What's going on behind the scenes at work that could affect my job?" Whatever your query, the *I Ching* is sure to provide an insightful answer.

The system is based on three-line patterns called trigrams, made of broken and unbroken lines. When two trigrams are stacked on top of each other, they form one of the sixty-four hexagrams that are the heart of the *I Ching*. To do a reading, think of a question and toss three coins; the way they fall determines the nature of your hexagram. The cosmic forces that are at work in your life will cause the coins to land in a certain position. Then translate the pattern of the coins and look up the meaning of the resulting hexagram, which is used as a guide to analyze your particular predicament.

The lines, trigrams, and hexagrams of the *I Ching* are based on the concept of yin and yang, which posits that the universe is composed of complementary opposites that flow continuously into one another, like day into night into day. Basically, yang is associated with firm-

ness, strength, and movement, while yin is associated with receptivity, openness, and flexibility. Balance comes from the rhythmic give-and-take between yin and yang.

The hexagram patterns are composed of the sixty-four possible six-row combinations of solid and broken lines. The solid lines represent yang and the broken lines represent yin. Each of the hexagrams is split into its upper and lower three-line trigrams. There are eight trigrams. When the trigrams are placed on top of one another in pairs, they form the six-line hexagrams. The lower trigram (bottom three lines of the hexagram) represents the internal, as-yet-undeveloped element of the situation. The upper trigram (top three lines) represents the external, or dominant, element of the situation. Think of it this way: The upper trigram issues the edict; the lower trigram carries it out.

Consulting the *I Ching*
(Throw a Penny, Make a Change)

Ideally, the reading should be done at a table or other flat surface; you'll need three coins of the same type (pennies are thought to be lucky) as well as a pencil and a piece of paper. One side of the coin (heads) represents yang, which is designated by a solid line; the other side (tails) represents yin, designated by a broken line.

Pick up the coins and hold them in your hands while you concentrate on your question, which should be as clear and concise as possible. With the question firmly in mind, throw the coins. Two heads equal a solid (yang) line; two tails equal a broken (yin) line. If you throw three of a kind, it means that the line is changing into its opposite sign. Three heads indicates that your solid (yang) line is changing into a broken (yin) line. Likewise, three tails means your broken (yin) line is firming up into a solid (yang) line.

If you've thrown two heads, simply draw a solid line; for two tails, draw a broken line. If you got three of a kind, indicate that the line is changing by making an arrow at the end of it. So, a regular solid (two heads) line would look like this: ──; a regular broken (two tails) line would look like this: ── ──; a changing (three heads) solid line looks like this: ──→; and a changing (three tails) broken line looks line this: ── ──→. After you've drawn your first line, repeat the procedure five more times until you've made a six-line hexagram (remember to focus on the question each time you toss the coins).

The only thing you need to know about building a hexagram is that the lines are drawn from the bottom up, like a ladder—the second line goes above the first line, the third line goes above the second line, and so on. Once you've constructed your hexagram, look it up using the Master Chart. Once you have located the number of your hexagram, turn to the appropriate page and read the main description provided. If you don't have any changing lines, you're done, and you can go on to ask another question for clarification or details. If you have changing lines, read the

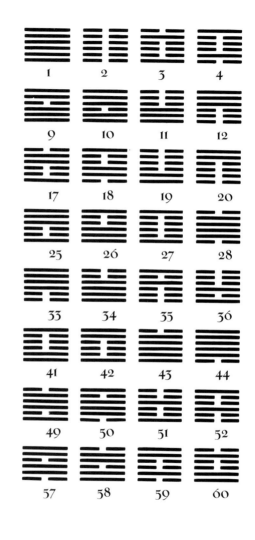

1   2   3   4

9   10   11   12

17   18   19   20

25   26   27   28

33   34   35   36

41   42   43   44

49   50   51   52

57   58   59   60

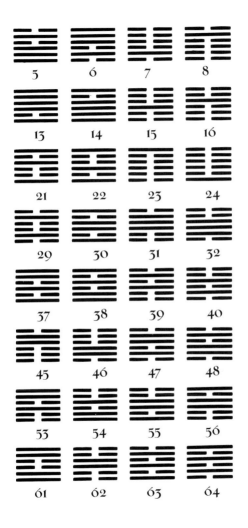

5	6	7	8
13	14	15	16
21	22	23	24
29	30	31	32
37	38	39	40
45	46	47	48
53	54	55	56
61	62	63	64

main description first. This will give you a general overview of what's going on. Then look up the descriptions for any and all changing lines. These will give you tips, provide extra information, and suggest the best way to proceed to affect the outcome of this particular situation.

Finally, convert your changing lines into their opposites—solid into broken and broken into solid—to create a new hexagram. Let's say your original hexagram was 16 (Thunder/Earth) with the second and fourth lines changing (remember to count from the bottom up). You'd first read the main description of hexagram 16, along with the descriptions of Changing Lines two and four. Then you'd convert these changing lines into their opposites to derive the final hexagram (hexagram #7, Earth/Water). Under that entry, read only the main description, which will enhance your understanding of the present situation and show you how things can be expected to turn out, given their current course.

If you had no changing lines, your situation is rather stable (at least for now); if they're *all* changing, the situation is about to undergo a complete reversal. Most hexagrams fall somewhere in between, and have one, two, or three changing lines. In reading the answers, you should focus on the lines that are changing, because these changes create the new hexagram which represents a new situation. Think carefully about the information and suggestions that are imparted by the changing lines; these will enable you to influence the outcome of the current goings-on and to take control of your future.

6

The value of the readings is largely dependent on how good you are at implementing the advice it gives. Don't be afraid to read between the lines (so to speak) and to draw your own conclusions. After all, it's *your* life. Only you can interpret the meaning of the hexagrams to see how they apply to your unique situation.

THE HEXAGRAMS

1.CH'IEN/THE CREATIVE (Heaven/Heaven)

This hexagram indicates unlimited creative potential and self-fulfillment. If you are receptive to the forces that surround you and can remain focused on the task at hand, successful solutions will present themselves. If you remain humble and act honorably, your patience will be rewarded.

LINE 1: Sit tight; this is definitely not the time to act. Use this interlude to prepare yourself for the next step.

LINE 2: There's light at the end of the tunnel. Use this time to gather information.

LINE 3: This is a troublesome, anxious time. Stay focused on what you want to achieve, and work hard to make it happen.

LINE 4: A state of transition. There are many opportunities for advancement. Follow your heart; big risks can mean big payoffs.

LINE 5: You're in a great position to turn your dreams into reality, due in large part to your seemingly effortless ability to win friends and influence people.

LINE 6: As long as you don't let your ego run rampant, success is assured.

2. K'UN/THE RECEPTIVE (Earth/Earth)

This is the time to follow, not to lead. Concentrate on your ability to nurture and support others, and give it your all at work, regardless of whether or not your efforts are rewarded. Use this quiet period to soul-search.

LINE 1: Current events foreshadow what's just around the bend. Things look bright; let nature take its course.

LINE 2: Less is more. Don't fight the situation.

LINE 3: The spotlight is on someone else right now. Remain true to your own beliefs, even if they aren't popular.

LINE 4: Be wary of exposing your opinions or actions to the scrutiny of others.

LINE 5: Work toward the common good, and stop worrying about what's in it for you.

LINE 6: Things have progressed as far as they can in this direction, and they'll soon begin moving the other way. Focus on the positive.

3. CHUN/DIFFICULTY AT THE BEGINNING (Water/Thunder)

Expect a current endeavor to get off to a *slooow* start. Be patient, and persevere. Things may feel a bit out of control for a while, but this, too, shall pass. Remember: All good things come to (s)he who waits.

LINE 1: Your position is shaky. Stay put until you figure out exactly what it is you want.

LINE 2: Although a solution presents itself, it's not the best one. Hold out until a better option comes along.

LINE 3: You're anxious to move things along, but if you attempt to do so on your own, you're doomed to fail.

LINE 4: It's time to make your move. Joining forces with like-minded others will bring good fortune.

LINE 5: Chip away at a large problem bit by bit, and you'll reduce its size in no time.

LINE 6: Although you're knee-deep in a maddeningly frustrating situation, don't give up. Your hard work will pay off.

4. MÊNG/INEXPERIENCE

(Mountain/Water)

You're in over your head. While your innocent outlook does lend you a unique perspective, developing your expertise will help you approach the situation from a position of strength. By increasing your knowledge, you increase your chance of succeeding.

LINE 1: Contemplate the situation from every angle. When in doubt, ask those in the know to help you out.

LINE 2: Be patient toward those who are undertaking new responsibilities. External composure complements a will of iron.

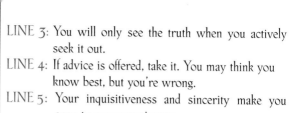

LINE 3: You will only see the truth when you actively seek it out.

LINE 4: If advice is offered, take it. You may think you know best, but you're wrong.

LINE 5: Your inquisitiveness and sincerity make you open to new experiences.

LINE 6: Let that be a lesson to you! Learn from past mistakes (your own as well as others').

5. HSÜ/WAITING (Water/Heaven)

What's your hurry? Timing is everything, and in this case, you'd do better to wait a while before proceeding. When it's time to move forward, you'll be the first to know. Stand by for now; patience is, indeed, a virtue.

LINE 1: There's trouble ahead. Stay calm, marshal your strength, and don't let the anticipation rattle you.

LINE 2: Remain calm in the face of the storm; it will be over as quickly as it began.

LINE 3: Impatience caused you to make your move too soon. Backtrack as fast as you can.

LINE 4: Concede gracefully. If you surrender first, your humility will win over your opponent.

LINE 5: A brief respite in the face of turmoil. Catch your breath, and wait to see what the outcome will be.

LINE 6: The solution that presents itself is not the one you had envisioned, but it represents a change, and that's just what you need.

6. SUNG/CONFLICT (Heaven/Water)

This imports dissension or strife. Confrontation is almost certain to occur, and you're not coming from a position of strength. If it's possible to avoid this situation, do so. If it isn't, proceed with caution. Compromise if need be, and maintain an aura of neutrality.

LINE 1: Conflict can be averted if you back off before things escalate further. Act with humility, and you'll emerge victorious.

LINE 2: Your opponent has the upper hand. Retreat while you can.

LINE 3: You're in an insecure position and feel threatened as a result. Rely on strategies that have worked for you in the past.

LINE 4: Things aren't going your way. Rise above it, and concentrate on putting your life back in order.

LINE 5: Your grievances are justified, and you are given the opportunity to settle disputes in a fair and responsible manner.

LINE 6: You may achieve a temporary gain by pushing your advantage unfairly, but this ill-gotten victory will soon unravel.

7. SHIH/THE ARMY (Earth/Water)

The present situation requires teamwork and team spirit. Mutual interests should be stressed to avoid conflict. Maintain your integrity, and keep your ego in check. If you

act in a humane manner, others will react accordingly.

LINE 1: Map things out ahead of time. Practice modesty, generosity, and discipline.

LINE 2: Your dedication and devotion to service are held in high esteem by those who count.

LINE 3: Incompetent leadership leads to disorder and disarray. Are you a good leader, or is it time that you stepped aside?

LINE 4: Step back, marshal your forces, and rethink your strategy.

LINE 5: It's your turn to delegate responsibility; match task to temperament. The goal is in sight.

LINE 6: You did it! Lasting progress comes through hard work and honorable intentions.

8. PI/UNION (Water/Earth)

Things are coming together. You need to hold your own and not lose sight of your principles in order to reach a goal. Cooperation is essential; a loyal community of friends or colleagues who can depend on each other is vital. The whole is greater than the sum of its parts.

LINE 1: If you approach others with sincerity, they will be drawn to you and will respond in kind.

LINE 2: You're on the inside track. Don't allow yourself to be misled; self-reliance is key.

LINE 3: Don't align yourself with dishonorable people. Reestablish your independence.

LINE 4: People outside the core group offer or need support; your cooperation benefits everyone.

LINE 5: Give others the room they need to maintain a sense of independence, and they'll be there for you when you need them.

LINE 6: A relationship not based on a shared truth is an ephemeral union.

9. HSIAO CH'U/THE NURTURE OF THE SMALL (Wind/Heaven)

Small stumbling blocks will impede (but not prevent) your progress. You'll achieve your goal more quickly if you don't rail against current restraints. Pay attention to your hunches; they can help prevent problems.

LINE 1: Trying to force a change will only hinder your advancement.

LINE 2: Enlist the cooperation of someone else when you wrestle with a problem.

LINE 3: Blaming others when things go wrong is not the solution; it will only serve to make a bad situation worse.

LINE 4: A calm, gentle approach will do wonders in diffusing a potentially explosive situation.

LINE 5: If you share your wealth with those who need it, you'll be doubly blessed.

LINE 6: The storm has passed, and success is imminent. Don't rush ahead: Take time to renew your resources; then move forward slowly.

10. LÜ/TREADING (Heaven/Lake)

This is a warning to proceed carefully. Before you try to move forward, take stock of just where you stand. Adopt a humble attitude. This situation does contain an element of danger.

LINE 1: Overweening ambition can only lead to your downfall. Keep things simple.

LINE 2: Acceptance of the situation leads to contentment. Remain detached from the conflicts of others.

LINE 3: You're pushing your luck, and it's not worth the risk. Make a hasty retreat.

LINE 4: Now's the time for risk-taking. Maneuver carefully, and you'll survive anything that gets in your way.

LINE 5: Don't start what you can't finish. Avoid involvement with the conflicts of others; let them learn from their mistakes.

LINE 6: Not sure that you're headed in the right direction? Take time to reflect. If you're reassured, continue on your present path. If not, sit for a while, and mull things over.

11. T'AI/PEACE (Earth/Heaven)

This is a wonderfully harmonious period, and everything is as it should be. Be assured that if you let events follow their natural course, everything will proceed smoothly, and you will experience personal growth as a result.

LINE 1: Your energy is directed outward, enabling favorable connections. A good time to act.

LINE 2: You'll need the support of others to survive a difficult transition. Don't let a difficult person or situation drag you down.

LINE 3: If you maintain your sense of inner peace, and act honorably, you'll easily rise above the fray.

LINE 4: You may not be able to pull this off on your own. Ask for assistance in a sincere, heartfelt way.

LINE 5: This is an auspicious time to forge partnerships of any kind.

LINE 6: Let go of the past. The end of one thing ultimately leads to the start of something new (and isn't that just what you need right now?).

12. P'I/STAGNATION (Heaven/Earth)

Progress has come to a halt. If you want to get moving again, you'll have to roll up your sleeves and get down to work. If there are other parties involved, meet them halfway, or you'll be stuck here forever. Above all, keep your chin up and stay true to your own guiding principles.

LINE 1: If you act quickly, you can nip a potentially disastrous situation in the bud.

LINE 2: You may have to flatter someone to get what you want. As unpleasant as that may be, it's the only solution available right now.

LINE 3: This is not the time to act like something you're not for the benefit of others. Remain true to yourself and your convictions.

LINE 4: Your potential is virtually unlimited, and the situation is improving by the minute.

LINE 5: Your confidence is at an all-time high. If your actions are well intentioned, you'll be amply rewarded.

LINE 6: Mission accomplished. You kept your head high and your nose to the grindstone during a troublesome episode, and your perseverance paid off.

13. T'UNG JÊN/FELLOWSHIP
(Heaven/Fire)

Your relationships can provide a clue to what needs to be done in the present situation. Friendly alliances will steer you toward magnificent success. Give your trust and companionship to those who earn it; remain polite, but keep your distance from those who aren't trustworthy.

LINE 1: Keep an open mind when meeting people for the first time. Don't engage in duplicity if you want to form a relationship that's based on trust.

LINE 2: Choose your friends carefully and for the right reasons—not because they curry favor.

LINE 3: Friendships based on hidden agendas are not worthwhile, and they will eventually lead to dissension and disintegrate.

LINE 4: If you take the high road, others will follow, and you'll soon realize your goal.

LINE 5: Getting everything out in the open now will only make you and a partner closer in the long run. The separation is temporary.

LINE 6: Be up front and honest in your dealings with other people, and you'll forge valuable new alliances.

14. TA YU/PROSPERITY (Fire/Heaven)

Now that you have found fulfillment (monetary, emotional, and professional), it's time to spread the wealth to those less fortunate than yourself. Feeling especially blessed, you're happy to share these blessings with others. Doing so will only increase your sense of well-being.

LINE 1: Your peace of mind and good fortune may be threatened. Behave in a humane, thoughtful manner, and people will respond in kind.

LINE 2: If you maintain your inner sense of balance and equanimity, you can navigate any circumstance with ease.

LINE 3: Do good for the sake of doing good, and you'll be amply rewarded.

LINE 4: It's not good manners to brag about your great good fortune. Be magnanimous toward other people.

LINE 5: If you want to influence other people, approach them without guile. Truthful sincerity will go a long way.

LINE 6: You are truly blessed in all areas of your life. Be thankful for this miraculous turn of events.

15. CH'IEN/HUMILITY (Earth/Mountain)

You'll advance more quickly if you employ modesty rather

than aggression. This situation is evolving steadily, although progress is hard to see. Don't try to force things; let nature take its course. Any display of ego or temperament would do more harm than good right now.

LINE 1: Your quiet confidence and self-discipline ensure success.

LINE 2: You come by your humility honestly. Other people recognize this and are drawn to you because of it.

LINE 3: Do whatever it takes to get the job done. Toil humbly, and you'll achieve the desired result.

LINE 4: Don't use humility as an excuse for inertia. It's possible to do what needs to be done and still remain modest.

LINE 5: It's time to move forward with determination, although you may encounter a slippery slope ahead. Action is imperative.

LINE 6: If you step forward now, others will fall in line behind you. It is possible to combine leadership qualities with humility.

16. YÜ/ENTHUSIASM (Thunder/Earth)

This is a particularly happy and harmonious interval; you are at one with the universe. You are feeling especially motivated and energetic; it's time to put your plan into action. If your motives are pure, you will meet with great success.

LINE 1: If you set your sights too high, you will be disappointed. Expect nothing, and you'll be content with anything.

LINE 2: Your persistence pays off. Maintain your integrity, be true to your principles, and victory will be yours. Action is called for.

LINE 3: If you want something done right, you have to do it yourself.

LINE 4: People view you as a source of inspiration. Use your influence to steer them onto the right path.

LINE 5: Don't allow others to bear the brunt of your laziness. If you don't pull your own weight, you may soon find that *you* have to answer to *them*.

LINE 6: Your enthusiasm has led you astray. Reconsider, implement a new plan, and all will not be lost.

17. SUI/FOLLOWING (Lake/Thunder)

There are several choices facing you. Weigh each possibility carefully; scrutinize it, and examine it from all angles. Then choose what works for you. One caveat: Before you leap, look to the example of others as a guide.

LINE 1: You suffer a slight setback; don't let it throw you. Stay the course if you want to overcome this problem. Listen to others.

LINE 2: Don't hold fast to an outmoded or subpar principle or person. Sometimes you have to let the little things go in order to make room for the big things.

LINE 3: Success is at hand, but a sacrifice is in order if you want to achieve your ultimate goal.

LINE 4: You got what you wanted. Now quit while you're ahead, or you risk inciting the ire (and envy) of others.

LINE 5: Success comes from adhering to your morals and principles (especially when you're inclined to do otherwise).

LINE 6: You're feeling constrained; but if you walk the moral high ground, you won't want for anything.

18. KU/REPAIR (Mountain/Wind)

Before you can move forward, you must settle old scores and repair what's been broken. Take responsibility for any damage you've caused, and fix what needs to be fixed. In the end, you'll feel better about both yourself and the situation. Your hard work brings good fortune.

LINE 1: By letting go of negative or destructive behavior, we allow our higher instincts to take root and flourish.

LINE 2: In this case, there is little you can do to rectify the situation. Face your fear, and you will ultimately triumph.

LINE 3: You're trying too hard to right old wrongs. Your impatience is understandable, but rest assured that everything will work out for the best.

LINE 4: You must confront the situation head-on if you want to put it behind you and move on.

LINE 5: You may be pressured to turn a blind eye to an ongoing problem, but don't give in. Help the person who really needs your help.

LINE 6: If your motivation is pure, and if your objective is noble, follow your instincts.

19. LIN/APPROACH (Earth/Lake)

There is concrete proof that you're closing in on your goal. Let intuition guide you on the road to success. Your insights and ideas are so inspired that they take your breath away. Stay focused; there's still work to be done.

LINE 1: Maintain your composure and integrity when you deal with people. Don't let ambition undermine your self-control.

LINE 2: Out with the old, in with the new! You'll handily dispatch any resistance you encounter. Don't fight what you can't change.

LINE 3: To be complacent and irresponsible during a crisis is to invite disaster. If you act quickly, catastrophe can be avoided.

LINE 4: Delegate responsibility if you want to achieve success. People are swayed by your honesty.

LINE 5: Doing something for the wrong (that is, selfish or unethical) reasons will ultimately lead to failure. Listen to your heart.

LINE 6: If you act in a righteous, magnanimous manner, you will have a positive influence on other people.

20. KUAN/CONTEMPLATION
(Wind/Earth)

Stop and take stock of where you are and where you're headed. To lay your anxieties to rest, you need a detached, balanced state of mind. Slow down and take a deep breath. Rush ahead blindly, and you will not achieve the desired result.

LINE 1: Free your mind. In your heart of hearts, you know what beliefs are morally correct; use this knowledge to enlighten others.

LINE 2: When you are comfortable enough to take a stand, pluck up your courage and let your voice be heard.

LINE 3: Examine your own thoughts and actions—past and present—to understand the current turn of events and to improve yourself.

LINE 4: Just because everyone does it, doesn't make it right. Those who adhere to decent principles can help others become more tolerant.

LINE 5: Work on bettering your own less than stellar attitude before you start worrying about other people's character flaws.

LINE 6: Acting in a sincere, tolerant, blameless manner will enrich your life immeasurably. Engage in some profound self-reflection.

21. SHIH HO/BITING THROUGH

(Fire/Thunder)

If you want to leap the hurdles before you, you'll need to act in a deliberate, decisive fashion. This is one problem you'll have to tackle head-on. Don't let peer pressure lead you astray; stick to your guns, even though you'll encounter much resistance.

LINE 1: In the initial stages, someone (or something) prevents you from making a mistake. Learn from this experience.

LINE 2: It's obvious that someone is not being forthright or truthful. Remain calm. If you're neutral, the situation will rectify itself.

LINE 3: Any attempt to lay blame or seek vengeance will only cause more hard feelings. If you're feeling vindictive, let it lie.

LINE 4: Approach the situation in a way that's fair and balanced, persevere, and you will be triumphant.

LINE 5: Your determination has been rewarded. If you place too much emphasis on this prize, however, misfortune will follow.

LINE 6: You let your ego get the upper hand, and it has cost you. Listen to the advice of others.

22. PI/GRACE (Mountain/Fire)

This is a presage to success. Simplicity is the best approach to any dilemma. Work on cultivating your inner strength and your sense of graciousness toward others. Behave thoughtfully rather than aggressively. Acceptance is the key.

LINE 1: Diligent effort guarantees that the end result will be that much more meaningful to you. Consider the views of others.

LINE 2: You look *mah-ve-lous*. Take pride in your superior qualities (inside and out), but don't get vain.

LINE 3: If you want to have a positive impact, you will have to get involved. Act with confidence.

LINE 4: Don't put up a false front if you want to gain the trust of others. Honesty will lead to success.

LINE 5: Your attributes may be modest, but they are laudable. Small gifts given with good intention are always well received.

LINE 6: In this case, less is definitely more. By eschewing overadornment, you gain real power and enlightenment.

23. PO/DISRUPTION (Mountain/Earth)

You're trapped in an upsetting, no-win situation. There is nothing you can do to affect the outcome of this particular event. Cultivate a good-natured, optimistic outlook, and ride it out. Eventually, the situation will reverse itself, and you'll have your day in the sun.

LINE 1: Things are beginning to disintegrate. Don't let fear or anxiety cause you to act rashly, or the situation will only get worse.

LINE 2: Chaos reigns. Bide your time patiently, and a solution will present itself. Be sure the people you're trusting to assist you are reliable.

LINE 3: Don't succumb to the unsavory influences of other people. Keep in mind what is morally correct, and act accordingly.

LINE 4: This is a *very* dangerous period; act carefully and cautiously. Don't resist change.

LINE 5: Humbly accept that your destiny is out of your hands right now.

LINE 6: Those who adhere to proper principles will be afforded a fresh start. Those who fixate on superficial ideals will not survive.

24. FU/RETURN (Earth/Thunder)

A dark period draws to a close and is replaced by a spring-like season of renewal and rebirth. Let things develop at their own pace, and accept what comes your way. Something you thought was lost forever reappears unexpectedly.

LINE 1: You've only gone a short distance out of your way, so returning to your original objective is easy. No harm done.

LINE 2: Don't indulge your ego. Treat people with tolerance and consideration if you want to restore harmony.

LINE 3: You keep repeating the same behavior (or returning to the same situation) over and over again. Why? Take time for reflection.

LINE 4: Let your intuition and higher principles be your guide. You may find yourself alone as a result, but it's the right thing to do.

LINE 5: Some critical self-examination is in order. Work on improving your character. Quash negative habits.

LINE 6: If you diverge from the path of righteousness, trouble will follow.

25. WU WANG/INNOCENCE
(Heaven/Thunder)

This is the culmination of a series of unseen events. The outcome may not be what you expected—surprise plays a big part in this situation—but things will work out in your favor if you expect nothing and accept everything.

LINE 1: Action wrought by good intentions will ultimately succeed.

LINE 2: Throw yourself into the task at hand without regard to reward, and your efforts will meet with success.

LINE 3: You feel responsible for a misfortune, even though it really wasn't your doing. Maintain your innocence, and don't try to force anything.

LINE 4: This is a time of transformation; you may feel alienated or powerless, but if you remain true to your principles, you'll be fine.

LINE 5: Trouble will take care of itself. If you try to fix things, you'll only make it worse.

LINE 6: If your efforts have been thwarted, take a breather while you map out a plan of attack.

26. TA CH'U/RESTRAINT

(Mountain/Heaven)

Take small, deliberate steps. Progress is slow, but steadfast perseverance will be met with success. There is great potential for power if you act wisely.

LINE 1: There's trouble a-brewing. Any attempt to mete out punishment to wrongdoers will fail. Accept the situation.

LINE 2: Railing against the Powers That Be will only sap your much-needed strength. Accept what you cannot control.

LINE 3: Don't pander to your lesser instincts. Embrace modesty and neutrality if you want to succeed.

LINE 4: Tantrums won't get you what you want. Settle down and conduct yourself with dignity; everything will happen in due course.

LINE 5: You're able to disarm a potentially destructive situation by acting with compassion and empathy.

LINE 6: Your creative energy is at its peak, and you've surmounted all obstacles. Sit back and enjoy the view from up here.

27. I/NOURISHMENT (Mountain/Thunder)

The image of this hexagram is that of an open mouth, and it serves as a reminder that our bodies and souls require constant care and feeding. You're hungering after something. This situation requires careful scrutiny and no small measure of soul-searching. Desire is not the same as need.

LINE 1: You want for nothing, yet you're envious of others. Perhaps you should look inward for the fulfillment that you seek.

LINE 2: Don't align yourself with people or situations for the wrong reasons. Are they truly worthy of your involvement?

LINE 3: You're looking for a quick fix instead of searching for a long-term solution. What would it take to really satisfy this hunger? Think about it.

LINE 4: You're filling your needs in a way that's proper and justified, and others are compelled to help you.

LINE 5: You are the leader, but don't let this keep you from seeking assistance when needed.

LINE 6: You are the source of nourishment. Use this power to enlighten others and to exert a positive influence on them.

28. TA KUO/EFFORT (Lake/Tree)

You are overwhelmed by pressures and responsibilities, and you must employ willpower and a tireless effort to see things through. You may not be up to the job right now, but stick with it, and your perseverance will be rewarded.

LINE 1: Care and planning are required for this major undertaking. Be respectful toward those in influential positions.

LINE 2: This is a time of rebirth. Awareness and humility save the day. Power is matched by compassion; it's a fortuitous union.

LINE 3: The pressure threatens to bury you; seek help. If you attempt to go it alone, you'll be crushed.

LINE 4: Stay true to your principles, and others will fall in beside you. Your strength is returning, but take care not to overtax yourself.

LINE 5: There is a structural problem that requires your attention; ignore it at your own risk.

LINE 6: You have lost sight of just what it is you're supposed to be doing. Reassess. If your motivation is impure, revise your goal.

29. K'AN/THE ABYSS (Water/Water)

This is a dangerous time, replete with crises and unexpected pitfalls. The only way to get through it is to remain steadfast in your beliefs. Decisive action is called for, although any move you make should be carefully considered beforehand.

LINE 1: Repeating bad behavior results in grave misfortune. Reflect on this warning.

LINE 2: Your situation is precarious. Small, cautious steps will lead you to higher ground.

LINE 3: You are caught in the jaws of a lion, and there's no way to extricate yourself without being eaten alive. Play dead until he lets you go.

LINE 4: You're plucked from the path of an oncoming freight train just in the nick of time. Give sincere thanks where thanks are due.

LINE 5: The ground only *appears* to be firm and level; in reality, it's a quagmire. Small, careful steps will lead you to safety.

LINE 6: In striving to avoid the unavoidable, you've only succeeded in making matters worse. Remain calm and bide your time; you'll emerge unscathed.

30. LI/DEPENDENCE (Fire/Fire)

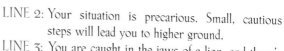

You must cling to proper principles in order to achieve spiritual awareness and enlightenment, and you must be honest in your relationships if you want them to flourish. Embrace and nurture the things that give you strength.

LINE 1: You're entering into an unfamiliar situation. Approach everything that comes with an open mind and a flexible attitude.

LINE 2: A supportive atmosphere fosters common goals. Think and act in a moderate, balanced matter. Everything is as it should be.

LINE 3: The sun has set (for now); nothing lasts forever.

It's better to accept this and move on. Tomorrow is the dawn of a new day.

LINE 4: Steadfast perseverance is met with success. Meandering from goal to goal leaves you exhausted, and it accomplishes nothing.

LINE 5: You are remorseful, and you express sincere regret for past wrongdoing. Do everything in your power to rectify these mistakes.

LINE 6: Weed out negative influences before they have a chance to take root and flourish.

31. HSIEN/INFLUENCE (Lake/Mountain)

This is a fortuitous period of give-and-take, an invigorating, renewing time. Share your ideas and enthusiams with other people, and take freely what they offer in return. Exhibit confidence, and act in an assured, decisive manner.

LINE 1: You're anxious to move on and to direct your energies outward. Proceed cautiously.

LINE 2: Jumping ahead too quickly has caused you to lose your footing. Regain your balance, and prepare to move when the time is right. Trust your intuition.

LINE 3: Figure out where you want to go before you start walking.

LINE 4: Remain calm in the face of the storm.

LINE 5: You know exactly what needs to be done; you just can't seem to make it happen. Stand your ground, but don't be inflexible.

LINE 6: Be careful not to say things you'll regret later. Your influence is at an all-time high; use it to assist or enlighten others.

32. HÊNG/PERSISTENCE (Thunder/Wind)

Constancy and endurance are the winning elements here. By standing firm, yet remaining flexible, the tree bends but does not break. Things are changing around you; don't lose sight of your ideals and guiding principles. Unyielding perseverance is the key to success.

LINE 1: Don't expect too much too soon. If you want something to last, it has to be painstakingly constructed. Give it some time.

LINE 2: Letting your ego run rampant would undermine any progress that's been made. Don't rage or despair if you're unable to express yourself fully. What's past is past; concentrate on the future.

LINE 3: Don't make promises you can't keep. Trying to measure up to outside expectations will only make you dissatisfied.

LINE 4: You are going about something in the wrong way. What is it that you really want? Figure it out, and invest your time wisely.

LINE 5: We are not responsible for the actions of others. Do what's right for you, and let other people take care of themselves.

LINE 6: You're feeling restless and anxious to move forward, but it's best to let things unfold in their own time. The use of force will result in misfortune.

33. TUN/RETREAT
(Heaven/Mountain)

The road to success is rife with twists and turns. This is a period of withdrawal from stress or conflicts. Keep your goal in sight, but take some private time to kick back and regain your strength. People, like plants, grow best when properly nurtured.

LINE 1: You can't win this one, so withdraw into quietude. Don't let your pride override your common sense.

LINE 2: A demand for rewards ensures the opposite outcome. Through steadfast determination, you will get what it is you desire—and deserve.

LINE 3: Avoid conflict. Focus on quieting your emotional turmoil and on cultivating the truth within yourself.

LINE 4: Continuous struggle against foes only strengthens their resolve. Step out of the ring.

LINE 5: You have reached your goal, and now it's time to call it a day. Pushing for more is both unseemly and potentially destructive.

LINE 6: You fought the good fight . . . and you won. Take your spoils, and retreat with grace and good cheer.

34. TA CHUANG/POWER OF THE GREAT (Thunder/Heaven)

You are in a position of power, and you have the ability to hold sway over other people. Use this influence wisely; it carries with it a great responsibility. You are determined to make things happen, and you have the means to carry out your plan.

LINE 1: Hold your horses! Still your raging ego, and regain your composure. It would not be in your best interest to act now.

LINE 2: The power is beginning to shift in your favor. Remain modest, and work steadily toward your goal.

LINE 3: There is no need for a vulgar display of power. Wait until you see an opening, then take it.

LINE 4: An opportunity presents itself. Work slowly and steadily, and you can overcome the obstacles in your path.

LINE 5: It's not wise to try to hold on to someone who's ready to move on. Let nature take its course.

LINE 6: Don't bully others into submission; a gentle touch is what's needed here. Given time, the situation will take care of itself.

35. CHIN/PROGRESS (Fire/Earth)

Smooth sailing. You're moving forward at quite a clip, and Lady Luck is riding shotgun. The time is right to finish a current project or to undertake a new one. You have the golden touch right now. Use it to your advantage; it won't last forever.

LINE 1: You are not yet confident enough to get what you want without compromise. Quiet determination will bring success.

LINE 2: Your progress is impeded by the actions of a jealous person. Don't despair; employ quiet perseverance.

LINE 3: A will of iron is most beneficial if it's tempered by an adaptable nature.

LINE 4: Progress has slowed a bit, but don't try to force events. Employ honesty and humility in your dealings with others.

LINE 5: You win some, you lose some. Concentrate on the goal ahead. Follow your heart, and you'll get there in no time.

LINE 6: If you want to salvage this situation, act aggressively. Return to more moderate behavior only when your objective has been met.

36. MING I/DARKNESS (Earth/Fire)

This is a period of confusion and misunderstanding. You're experiencing some serious doubts, and you feel very much alone and abandoned. Remember: What goes around, comes around. Persevere, and you will emerge into daylight once again.

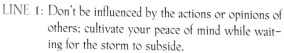

LINE 1: Don't be influenced by the actions or opinions of others; cultivate your peace of mind while waiting for the storm to subside.

LINE 2: You get caught in a squall. Not to worry; your injuries are minor. Help yourself by helping others in need.

LINE 3: If you see a wrong, move quickly to set it right. Although you succeed in correcting the problem, improvements won't be felt for quite a while. But there is light at the end of the tunnel.

LINE 4: Remain true to your beliefs, and you'll emerge unscathed. Stay in this unsavory situation too long, and you'll live to regret it.

LINE 5: You're running with the wrong crowd. Refuse to participate in the destruction, and maintain your inner strength.

LINE 6: Everything is coming to a head. Stay balanced, and accept whatever happens; you're almost out of the dark.

37. CHIA JÊN/FAMILY (Wind/Fire)

You feel connected to other people, and they to you. Nurture this warm, supportive atmosphere, and nurture those qualities within yourself (empathy, serenity, tolerance, humility) that draw out the best in others.

LINE 1: Stay home and lock the doors if you're feeling threatened. Compromise when necessary.

LINE 2: Duties outweigh personal desires right now. Stick close to home, and fulfill your obligations.

LINE 3: You must be firm, yet flexible, if you want to maintain a sense of balance and harmony.

LINE 4: Allow other people to contribute what they can. Peace of mind is the result of a balanced, compassionate outlook.

LINE 5: Admirable characteristics increase your influence and power. The situation is harmonious; family members are in accord with one another.

LINE 6: Self-reliance is key right now. If you are principled in thought and action, everything will fall into place.

38. K'UEI/OPPOSITION (Fire/Lake)

Your closest relationship has undergone a transformation. You're suddenly estranged, and you feel as though you've been left out in the cold. A sense of doubt and alienation clouds everything you do. A reconciliation must take place before you can move forward. Inspiration strikes when you need it most.

LINE 1: You cannot force closeness. Face your fears, and meet your partner halfway, while remaining true to your own beliefs.

LINE 2: A relationship becomes strained when the partners cannot see eye to eye. Approach the matter in an open, casual manner.

LINE 3: It feels as though the forces of the universe are plotting against you. Accept what comes with grace, and good fortune will follow.

LINE 4: You feel isolated and alone. Seek out like-minded people in a sincere, open manner. Trust blossoms when you're honest.

LINE 5: Don't let a misunderstanding obscure the truth and ruin a worthwhile relationship. Stop allowing fear to dampen your sense of fun and adventure.

LINE 6: Lay down your weapon, and raise the white flag. Mistrust gives way to happy relief when you realize your mistake.

39. CHIEN/OBSTRUCTION

(Water/Mountain)

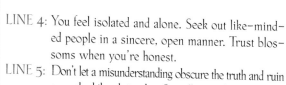

Careful attention to detail and concentrated, deliberate effort are necessary to put problems behind you. Self-examination provides the strength and insight you'll need to overcome this situation. Slog onward, and your perseverance will be duly rewarded.

LINE 1: Don't move a muscle until you're sure the time is right. Wait and watch.

LINE 2: Someone else made a mess and left it for you to clean up. It's not fair, but it has to be done. Go to it!

LINE 3: The road ahead is littered with hurdles, and you're in no position to jump them. Help will arrive in due time.

LINE 4: Slow down and gather your strength before moving forward. When the time is right, you'll be shown how to proceed.

LINE 5: A friend arrives to offer assistance just in the nick of time! Disaster is averted.

LINE 6: Look inward for the solutions you seek. Offer a helping hand (or a word of advice) to those who need it.

40. HSIEH/OPPORTUNITY (Thunder/Water)

Deliverance: You've licked the problems that have besieged you recently. If you still have a ways to go, press forward, and you'll make real headway in reaching your goal. This is a transformational period—the first step in establishing a brand-new, confident you. Aim high. Your reach will not exceed your grasp.

LINE 1: Act quickly to correct a problem before it gets out of hand. Remain vigilant and calm.

LINE 2: Don't indulge negative emotions and lowly ideals. If you labor on the path of goodness, your loftiest ambition will be fulfilled.

LINE 3: Acting in a vain or condescending manner will only set you up for a humiliating fall.

LINE 4: Extricate yourself from a sticky situation before it's too late.

LINE 5: Your upstanding character sets a great example for others. Use this influence to create a supportive, cooperative environment.

LINE 6: Ask an objective outsider to intervene in a troublesome situation. Renounce egotism.

41. SUN/REDUCTION (Mountain/Lake)

Get rid of the unrewarding activities and people in your life, and make room for the things that truly are valuable. Purge yourself of negative attitudes and self-destructive behaviors. Use this time for quiet contemplation and reflection. Get in touch with the higher aspects of your being.

LINE 1: Offer help without seeking rewards or adulation in return. Be empathetic and gentle.

LINE 2: You must help yourself before you can help others. Assist only those whose motivations and impulses are pure.

LINE 3: Put your own needs aside for the good of the group. Ask for guidance when it is appropriate.

LINE 4: You're working like a dog to change your present situation, but this will only tire you out. Slow down, and let your problems work themselves out.

LINE 5: By eliminating the negative influences in your life, you've made room for a wonderful new opportunity. Jump at it!

LINE 6: Sharing your newfound balanced attitude with others will only increase your good fortune.

42. I/INCREASE (Wind/Thunder)

This is a highly auspicious period of tremendous progress and accumulation (physical, emotional, and spiritual). Enjoy it, but keep pushing forward; you've built up unstoppable momentum, and you can achieve anything you put your mind to right now. This is a great opportunity; make the most of it.

LINE 1: It's time to put your plan into action. If you undertake an ambitious project now, you'll handily dispatch any opposition.

LINE 2: You may be given an unexpected gift or opportunity. Accept it in the benevolent spirit in which it was given.

LINE 3: An unfortunate or difficult situation can be used to your advantage. Adhere to proper principles and you will benefit without causing harm to others.

LINE 4: You are entrusted with an important task, and you carry it out with grace. An influential person can be a helpful intermediary.

LINE 5: When kind consideration comes from the heart and is motivated by selflessness and love, it is recognized as such.

LINE 6: Help those less fortunate than yourself. If you persist in being greedy and selfish, you leave yourself open to attack.

43. KUAI/SELF-DISCIPLINE, DETERMINATION (Lake/Heaven)

Pressures are mounting. It's time to confront the problem at hand before it explodes. Deal with it openly and honestly. Brute force and negativity won't get you as far as persever-

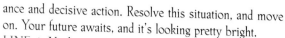

ance and decisive action. Resolve this situation, and move on. Your future awaits, and it's looking pretty bright.

LINE 1: You're anxious to proceed, but there are still some hurdles ahead. You know your limits; don't push past them, or you'll fail miserably.

LINE 2: There is danger everywhere, but if you're prepared, you can easily ward it off. Stay alert, and you'll be ready for anything.

LINE 3: Do not allow yourself to be provoked into a rash, ill-timed action. Act in a fair, reasonable way.

LINE 4: Follow the crowd; it's time to hand over the reins to someone else and to allow yourself to be led— at least for a while.

LINE 5: Stay the course. Don't indulge inferior influences or people. Remain true to your ideals.

LINE 6: Trouble may rear its ugly head unexpectedly. Take the time to right an old wrong, and you'll achieve your goal.

44. KOU/MEETING (Heaven/Wind)

Pay close attention to one-on-one relationships. A disruptive, unsettling influence may intrude and wreak havoc in your personal or professional affairs. Maintain your integrity; don't allow yourself to be seduced by lowly influences (there is a strong sexual undercurrent here). Be ready for anything. Caution is advisable.

LINE 1: Quell destructive impulses before they get out of control. Hold to what is correct, and harmony will be restored.

LINE 2: It is unwise to sacrifice what you cannot spare. Resist the temptation to act out negative emotions; be patient, and they will subside.

LINE 3: Watch your back. Taking a stand right now will be risky at best, as you'll only get slapped down.

LINE 4: Other people may behave horrendously, but you are in no position to judge or condemn them. Remain loyal.

LINE 5: Adhere to correct principles, and others will be inspired to follow your lead. You don't have to shout to be heard.

LINE 6: You may have to lock horns with someone whose bullheaded refusal to cooperate has you up against the wall. Let petty barbs and insinuations roll off your back, and comport yourself with dignity.

45. TS'UI/GATHERING (Lake/Earth)

Great strength is achieved when the members of a group are united toward a single purpose. Sacrifice your own needs for the common good. Cultivate the exemplary leadership qualities within yourself (fairness, flexibility, resolute dedication to the task at hand), then you will be in a position to guide others.

LINE 1: Initially, leadership gets under way with small, tentative steps. Your footing will become more secure with each forward step.

LINE 2: If you approach people sincerely, they will respond favorably to your offer of help (or they will offer you assistance).

LINE 3: You're feeling isolated and lonely, which may cause you to behave carelessly. The damage is slight, but it might be time to move on. This is a difficult transition, but your regrets are short-lived.

LINE 4: If you work for the greater good, you will be amply rewarded.

LINE 5: Respect isn't given; it's earned. Behave in a manner befitting your position, and people will fall in line behind you.

LINE 6: Oh, how the mighty have fallen. You have failed through no fault of your own. Accept defeat gracefully, and prepare to move on.

46. SHÊNG/ASCENSION (Earth/Wind)

You are pushing upward like a tree seeking sunlight. They say that timing is everything, and yours has been impeccable thus far. If you continue in this vein, you'll progress by leaps and bounds. Consult with people in positions of power. Your potential for growth is unlimited.

LINE 1: You're in line for a promotion, and the boss agrees that it's long overdue. Congratulations!

LINE 2: Give 110 percent to a current project. Superiors take note of your hard work and unwavering support, and they reward you.

LINE 3: There are no more obstacles between you and your goal; go for it!

LINE 4: Do whatever it takes to get the job done. An attitude adjustment may be in order if you can't put your professional duties before personal desires.

LINE 5: Advancement comes slowly. Just keep putting one foot in front of the other, and you'll get there eventually.

LINE 6: Darkness descends suddenly, and you can no longer see your goal. Don't panic—and don't lose heart. Just give your eyes a chance to adjust, then take small, measured steps (grope if you have to!).

47. K'UN/EXHAUSTION (Lake/Water)

You feel isolated, exhausted, oppressed, and depressed. In fact, you may be questioning the very nature of your existence. Hold fast to the inner truth deep within you. It's the only thing that will see you through this bleak time. Yes, you will get through it; this is a test.

LINE 1: Frustration and hopelessness are the prevalent emotions. Look inside yourself for inspiration, or seek help.

LINE 2: Your depression may be the result of unmet, unrealistic expectations. Stop focusing on what you don't have, and give thanks for what you have.

LINE 3: You're in a no-win situation, and you don't have the energy to extricate yourself. Stay calm, and wait for the storm to subside.

LINE 4: Progress has slowed to a standstill due to your own presumption or to your misplaced confidence in another.

LINE 5: Don't give in to despair; a sacrifice or cooperative effort may salvage the situation.

LINE 6: The only real limitations are those you impose on yourself. This darkness is only an illusion.

48. CHING/RESOURCES (Water/Wind)

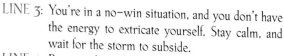

This is a time of sharing and mutual cooperation. Your resources are plentiful, and your options, abundant. Do not ignore this opportunity for personal and spiritual development. The well of life stands brimming before you . . . so *drink, already!*

LINE 1: If you don't adhere to correct behavior, the well becomes muddy and undrinkable. Return to proper principles and your resources will be replenished.

LINE 2: You are wasting your energies on worthless pursuits. Redirect your efforts.

LINE 3: Opportunity knocks. Don't let fear keep you from answering the door; you may never get another chance like this one.

LINE 4: The well has not been not properly maintained. Take time to repair the damage.

LINE 5: The well is in perfect working order; draw on its resources to nourish your body and spirit.

LINE 6: You allow others to benefit from your resources. This is fortuitous, as long as you preserve your source of strength.

49. KO/REVOLUTION (Lake/Fire)

This is a period of radical, transformative change. You are ready to shed old habits and behaviors that are no longer beneficial. Keep sight of your ultimate goal (nothing less than emotional and spiritual fulfillment), and you'll be back on track in no time. Remember: Timing is everything. It's an epic undertaking (and way, way overdue). Good luck to the new, improved you!

LINE 1: You do not have the strength or support to implement any changes just yet. Wait until an opening presents itself.

LINE 2: Change is possible if you are prepared. Move with quiet humility, and keep your ego in check.

LINE 3: If you move before the time is right, you will fail. Wait until you have received a clear signal, then push forward with confidence.

LINE 4: If you have faith in your goal, change can only be auspicious (and successful). Do not doubt the merit of your undertaking.

LINE 5: You accomplish change most effectively when you behave in an exemplary manner. Others support your selfless motivation.

LINE 6: You are in a position of influence and power. People will be drawn to your strength of purpose, and they will seek to imitate you.

50. TING/THE CAULDRON (Fire/Wind)

This is about cooking up new ways of doing things: new ideas, new approaches, new outlooks. Stir up and nourish the good within yourself; skim off and discard the bad. If used wisely, this fortuitous period of self-improvement can have far-reaching (and long-lasting) results, namely: balance, security, and peace of mind.

LINE 1: Rid yourself of negative thoughts and attitudes. We must sometimes employ questionable methods to achieve a desired result.

LINE 2: Your dream becomes a reality; confidence and self-reliance follow. Remain true to your principles.

LINE 3: Foolish pride has caused you to miss an opportunity. But a second chance will be offered.

LINE 4: Your honesty has been called into question, causing a potential opportunity to be lost forever. Continue to neglect your responsibilities and you will suffer gravely.

LINE 5: Past transgressions have been forgiven and forgotten. Your balance and open-mindedness are justly rewarded.

LINE 6: A very auspicious time. You combine the best of yin and yang: firm flexibility. You are a fine example for others.

51. CHÊN/SHOCK (Thunder/Thunder)

An arousing, invigorating, and energizing situation. You're in for a few shocks yourself. They may be inspiring, or they may be unsettling—it all depends on your point of view. Stay close to the ground if you don't want to get hit.

LINE 1: A surprise can leave us frightened at first, but it's beneficial if we learn something. A scream, followed by relieved laughter.

LINE 2: A storm approaches, causing you to put down your valuables and run. You'll regain what you've lost once the threat has subsided.

LINE 3: You act with uncharacteristic impetuousness, but because it is tempered with self-control, you are successful in your endeavor.

LINE 4: Your progress is slowed by muddy thinking. Don't resist the situation; accept what is happening, and you'll learn a valuable lesson.

LINE 5: Stay centered, and keep moving toward your destination; you won't be struck down.

LINE 6: People around you are in danger, but you are safe from harm. Aggressive action is not as beneficial as passive resistance.

52. KÊN/STILLNESS (Mountain/Mountain)

Timing is everything. Change cannot be forced right now, so just observe and accept events as they unfold around you. You will know the right time to act. Stay put until then, and concentrate on self-reflection.

LINE 1: This is not the time to act. If you press forward, you're likely to make a wrong move. Hang back.

LINE 2: Don't let others goad you into action, as it will just cause trouble. If they insist on pushing forward, let them go it alone.

LINE 3: You can't will yourself to be cheerful or upbeat if a situation is not to your liking. Cultivate a sense of calm acceptance.

LINE 4: Behave with gentle humility. If you accept whatever comes your way, and calm your emotions, your thinking will remain calm as well.

LINE 5: Watch what you say; that mouth of yours could get you in hot water. Restraint and reticence are the order of the day.

LINE 6: There's no point in going any further than you have to; stop once you've reached your goal.

53. CHIEN/DEVELOPMENT
(Wind/Mountain)

You *are* moving forward; it just feels like you're standing still, because your progress has been so slow and gradual. It would be unwise to try to force matters with impetuous action. Determination and focused perseverance ensure success.

LINE 1: Don't let doubts undermine your confidence. Persevere, and you'll progress nicely.

LINE 2: You are no longer a beginner, and your self-assurance shows. Don't let it go to your head; share your good fortune with others.

LINE 3: Don't be drawn into unnecessary conflicts. Remain balanced, and work toward a mutually satisfying solution.

LINE 4: Railing against the Powers That Be will not prevent current events from unfolding. Retreat to a secure perch, and let nature take its course.

LINE 5: Your determination and persistence have finally paid off. Your time is at hand; make the most of it.

LINE 6: You have succeeded beyond your wildest dreams! Behave in a manner that befits a person of your stature, and you'll be an inspiration to all who cross your path.

54. KUEI MEI/CAUTION (Thunder/Lake)

This is not a fortuitous period. You may be tempted to bite off more than you can chew; doing so will only cause you to choke on your own greed and ambition. Mull over every decision thoughtfully and carefully before you make a move.

LINE 1: You're not in a position to move forward by leaps and bounds. Patiently await your turn; it'll be here before you know it.

LINE 2: At first glance, this certainly looks like a no-win situation. If you check your pessimism at the door, an opportunity will present itself in short order.

LINE 3: Indulging your ego will only cause despair. Your great expectations cannot be met right now.

LINE 4: All good things come to those who wait. You will reach your goal; it's just going to take longer than you originally had planned.

LINE 5: You've had your chance to shine; turn the spotlight over to someone else.

LINE 6: Your motives are questionable at best. Reconsider your attitude, and make the necessary adjustments.

55. FÊNG/ABUNDANCE (Thunder/Fire)

This is an unusually fulfilling time, ripe with possibility. Everything is running smoothly, and great progress is being made. You have worked long and hard, and everything has turned out even better than you expected. This period won't last forever, but you can prolong it if you do not indulge in excessive or ostentatious behavior.

LINE 1: An influential person offers help. Accept it, but don't depend on this person to be there forever.

LINE 2: Approach others in a friendly and sincere manner. If you act like a phony, you'll be treated like one. Hold fast to what is right.

LINE 3: You let your ego get the upper hand. Return to humble honesty, and the damage is easily repaired.

LINE 4: You're lost in the dark, and you cannot get your bearings. Let your eyes adjust to the darkness, and you'll spot a way out.

LINE 5: You are truly blessed. Others love, appreciate, and support you and everything you stand for. What more could you ask for?

LINE 6: If you refuse to share your wealth with others, downfall is inevitable. Don't wait until it's too late.

56. LÜ/WANDERING (Fire/Mountain)

You're in a transitory period. This is not the time for long-term planning. Enjoy your present surroundings; you'll find yourself on the right path soon enough. Behave magnanimously toward others despite your inner confusion and loneliness. Relax and enjoy the scenery; your final destination will become clear in time.

LINE 1: Remain detached. You've got places to go and people to see; don't allow yourself to get sidetracked along the way.

LINE 2: You've been welcomed with open arms: nice accommodations, good food, and the locals are friendly, too. It's a nice place to visit . . . so why don't you do just that (for a while, anyway).

LINE 3: Don't interfere in the affairs of others. If you can't hold your tongue, it's probably best to move on.

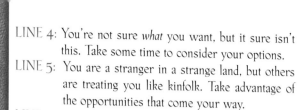

LINE 4: You're not sure *what* you want, but it sure isn't this. Take some time to consider your options.

LINE 5: You are a stranger in a strange land, but others are treating you like kinfolk. Take advantage of the opportunities that come your way.

LINE 6: If you behave carelessly or take things for granted, misfortune will follow. Do unto others... (it'll work like a charm).

57. SUN/SUBMISSION (Wind/Wind)

Keep your sights high and your mind open. It's always auspicious to adapt to our surroundings. If you're modest enough to accept advice and assistance from others, they can help you realize your goals. Flexibility allows you to bend without breaking.

LINE 1: Banish doubt and indecision by focusing on the task at hand. Advance only when you have a plan (and the strength to carry it out).

LINE 2: A powerful person is aware of your abilities and offers to help; you'd be a fool to refuse.

LINE 3: If there's a problem, fix it, and move on. Focusing on the negative will only hinder your progress (as will inflexibility).

LINE 4: You can remain true to your principles without alienating other people. Compromise is the key to success.

LINE 5: You've had your share of trouble, but things are beginning to look up. Make like a tree and bend; you'll be glad you did.

LINE 6: Work on improving your bad behavior, and you may be able to turn the situation around.

58. TUI/JOY (Lake/Lake)

Everything has gone according to plan, and you couldn't be happier (or more satisfied). Take pride in the fact that these accomplishments are due to your own hard work, determination, and exemplary behavior. It really doesn't get any better than this. Revel in it!

LINE 1: You are able to speak your mind openly. Freeing yourself from material desire brings joy.

LINE 2: Don't let momentary pleasures distract you from the task at hand. Be truthful when expressing your opinions and desires.

LINE 3: Sublimating your own needs to please someone else ultimately will backfire. Envy and unbridled ambition only interfere with your happiness.

LINE 4: You have more than enough; trying to keep up with others will only lead to unhappiness. Finish what you started.

LINE 5: Don't let others take advantage of you. Negative emotions cause disharmony; focus on the positive.

LINE 6: Accept things as they are; you can't save the world (although this shouldn't prevent you from living life to its fullest).

59. HUAN/DISPERSAL (Wind/Water)

Your energies are scattered, and you're having trouble concentrating on the task at hand. This is an unsettling, rather insecure period, but you are not without recourse and resources. Remain focused, and continue to work toward your goal. Remain flexible and nonjudgmental toward other people and toward the situation at large.

LINE 1: Nip misunderstandings in the bud. Ask a friend to help you extricate yourself from a potentially destructive situation.

LINE 2: You're not sure where the current situation is headed, but if you hang on for the ride, you're sure to be pleasantly surprised.

LINE 3: Don't be petty. If you want to get ahead now, you must first help other people.

LINE 4: It's time for a change. If something (or someone) conflicts with your ethics or principles, give 'em the old heave-ho.

LINE 5: Use your influence to promote the common good. Take the chance; take the risk; take the reins.

LINE 6: Focusing on negative emotions will only lead to misfortune. You narrowly escape a dangerous situation.

60. CHIEH/LIMITATIONS (Water/Lake)

This situation calls for discipline and restraint. You're feeling very organized and efficient; it's a good time to fulfill obligations and meet responsibilities. Just make sure you don't go overboard; moderation in all things will lead to success.

LINE 1: When you go looking for trouble, you're sure to find it. Know your limits, and don't push beyond them.

LINE 2: (S)he who hesitates misses a great opportunity. Take this offer; you won't get another chance.

LINE 3: Correct mistakes before they come back to haunt you. Are you big enough to admit when you're wrong? Do the right thing, regardless of what's in it for you.

LINE 4: Your routine (and self-discipline) have gotten you this far; no need to fix what isn't broken.

LINE 5: If you expect other people to play by the rules, you have to do the same.

LINE 6: Excessive limitations are counterproductive. You've pushed yourself too far, and you're exhausted as a result. Lighten up. If anyone deserves some rest, you do.

61. CHUNG FU/TRUTH (Wind/Lake)

If you are committed and sincere, others will want to follow your lead. Wholehearted honesty inspires confidence. Follow your heart, seek out the truth, and look inward for guidance and inspiration. You can accomplish great things through steadfast determination.

LINE 1: Your devotion to a higher cause gives you strength and stability. Be wary of a traitor in your midst.

LINE 2: Your inner state of being reflects out toward others

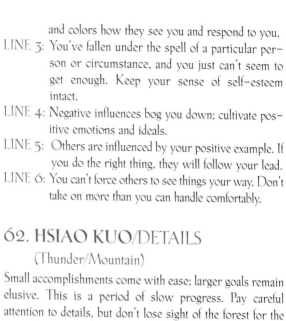

and colors how they see you and respond to you.

LINE 3: You've fallen under the spell of a particular person or circumstance, and you just can't seem to get enough. Keep your sense of self-esteem intact.

LINE 4: Negative influences bog you down; cultivate positive emotions and ideals.

LINE 5: Others are influenced by your positive example. If you do the right thing, they will follow your lead.

LINE 6: You can't force others to see things your way. Don't take on more than you can handle comfortably.

62. HSIAO KUO/DETAILS
(Thunder/Mountain)

Small accomplishments come with ease; larger goals remain elusive. This is a period of slow progress. Pay careful attention to details, but don't lose sight of the forest for the trees. Be content with modest gains; don't push your luck.

LINE 1: You're dying to make your move, but to do so augurs failure. Wait until the balance has shifted in your favor.

LINE 2: You're not in a position to realize all of your dreams, so be satisfied by what you're able to accomplish with such limited resources.

LINE 3: If you stick your neck out too far, you're liable to lose your head. Remain humble.

LINE 4: Don't act to gratify your ego. The situation you face is not without danger; exercise caution.

LINE 5: People will be happy to oblige if you ask for guidance. For now, lower your expectations, and content yourself with small gains.

LINE 6: Forcing an issue just digs you deeper into the hole.
Don't start something you cannot finish; you'll
only embarrass yourself.

63. CHI CHI/COMPLETION (Water/Fire)

A favorable period of accomplishment and unmitigated
success. Everything you touch turns to gold; every promise
is fulfilled. Keep in mind that once you've realized your
greatest ambition, it's time to turn your attention else-
where. Enjoy the present, but keep your eyes fixed firmly
on the horizon.

LINE 1: Don't ignore the rumblings of trouble; this is one
warning you should heed. Go one step at a time.

LINE 2: You can earn the respect and cooperation of other
people by behaving appropriately.

LINE 3: Don't take on too much now, or you'll lose whatever you've accomplished thus far.

LINE 4: If it looks like rain, bring an umbrella. Vigilance
can prevent careless slipups.

LINE 5: Behave with humble sincerity, and even your
smallest gestures will carry great weight.

LINE 6: So close and yet so far . . . If you stop to pat yourself on the back now, you'll fail. Keep going;
you're almost there.

64. WEI CHI/INCOMPLETION
(Fire/Water)

The outcome of your present situation is still up in the air. If you want to make a difference, there's still time left. You cannot force a change quickly, but through steady perseverance, you can affect how things play out.

LINE 1: Your enthusiasm caused you to jump before you were ready, and now the ice is breaking beneath your feet. Get back to shore as quickly as you can, and remain there until things become firm.

LINE 2: Don't venture out just yet, as trouble is lying in wait. Bide your time, and move once the coast is clear.

LINE 3: Although you're ready to proceed, you'll have to take two steps back before you can take a step forward.

LINE 4: Take decisive action when necessary, and keep on keeping on. If you pause for breath now, you may lose everything.

LINE 5: What goes around, comes around. Share your good fortune with others.

LINE 6: Your ego is running amuck. Stop mincing around, and roll up your sleeves; there's work to be done.